This guide can and should be used for

hemp! but we will refer all plants as

cannabis or marijuana. It is the readers

responsibility to conform with all laws

local and federal we do not advise

breaking the law in anyway. (no really)

Dedicated to Dr. Jones a Mother & role

model.

Section 1 Before starting

Preface

One of the most fascinating and rewarding plants to cultivate is undoubtedly marijuana, if only because it has a remarkably short lifespan. In only three to six months, you get to see the whole process from germination to harvest, and of course, when the process is done, you get to enjoy the fruits of your labor. Many potential growers may take the air of nonchalance to grow marijuana, but that's really not the way to go about it. It is a labor-intensive effort that will require you to take great care of the plants if by harvest time, you want the best product.

Although it can be quite intimidating, that doesn't mean it shouldn't be attempted at all. In fact, many people have been taking to cannabis cultivation who have no gardening or horticultural experience whatsoever. Some people believe that while you can't get addicted to the use of cannabis, you can definitely get addicted to growing cannabis. This guide for beginning

cultivation will definitely provide you
with a strong foundation to help make
growing your cannabis crop a much
simpler process overall.

Of course, as the murky legal history of
cannabis in the United States (and
indeed

around the world) would let you know,
growing cannabis carries a certain
degree of risk.

And states that have legalized recreational or medical use of cannabis also maintain stringent regulations about the actual growth of marijuana. As all states are different you should consult your local government to find out about any regulations regarding growing cannabis or hemp.

The curious thing about the legal status of cannabis in modern times is that the herb and humans have enjoyed a kind of symbiotic relationship for decades.

The plant has thrived as a result of cultivation, and humans have benefited from the medicinal effects of cannabis. Even so, until about century ago, marijuana was used in Western medicine as a method of treating all sorts of different diseases.

Unfortunately, many countries around the world have criminalized it despite the reality

that it is one of the most harmless substances you can use. It does not have the addictive properties of hard opioids such as cocaine or opium, and in some situations is much better than the use of widely used medications.

Chapter 1

Types of Marijuana

Cannabis is one of the few annual plants

with two separate sexes. This means

that plants may come from both male

and female varieties, and sometimes

even from hermaphrodite varieties, in

which the plant has both male and female reproductive organs. There are also three primary forms of marijuana.

Indica: Comparatively short and large, with greener colors and circular leaves with marble-like shapes. Provides a big, high body.

Sativa: Can grow taller, but smaller with more pointed leaves that have no pattern on them. Provides an energetic, cortical high

Ruderalis: less recognized among the other two. Small trees, mostly used to produce clothing, ropes, etc. It is also used to create auto flowering strains.

Each of these types of cannabis has its own qualities when it comes to actually consuming it.

A few of the main potency measures for a specific plant is its THC (tetrahydrocannabinol) and CBD (Cannabidiol) content. Essentially, this is the stuff that offers the calming, healing properties that many people equate with cannabis. In general, the majority of farmers use Indica, Sativa, or hybrid hybrids of both. Ruderalis is usually left out of the cultivation of cannabis because it lacks a large volume of THC and CBD. In addition, it should be remembered that the female sex in the cannabis plant is most appreciated by growers because of its higher THC and CBD content.

In the majority of female plants, THC and CBD grows while the plant stays unpollinated. It will produce more flowers, more buds, and more THC resin, making the smoke by the time of harvest even more potent. There are also a lot of other natural chemicals in a marijuana plant that influence the form and degree of high you get. These compounds are referred to as cannabinoids which interface with the cognitive and physical processes in order to create altered states of mind and becoming. Growing plants under ideal conditions will encourage the

production of high-quality THC in your

female plants. Indica/Sativa

crossbreeding's such as Skunk, Northern

Lights, Orange Bud and Blueberry are

very common.

Chapter 2

Cannabis Seeds

There are a variety of places to find marijuana seeds, but when you're in the United States, nearly all of them are unlawful (but google is always one step away). Of course, if your state has legalized growing of cannabis or hemp this will not be an issue and you will likely be able to source seeds or clones. Where you buy your seeds will likely depend on your location as each state varies in the regulation required by vendor. If you are purchasing hemp seeds your options are more varied as it has been made federally legal but you will need to make sure there are no restrictions on the shipment or possession of hemp seeds in your state. For inexperienced growers with knowledge with various marijuana strains, the position of a preferred strain is likely to be a priority. Most of the vendors categorize their seeds by strain.

They may have special names for their individual strains, but the genus (i.e. indica, sativa, etc) can show what you might anticipate from the smoke. In any case, it's important to find the seeds that best fit your smoking experience.

After obtaining your marijuana seeds, be sure to check your seeds for consistency. Many mature seeds have a dark brown hue with swirling or marbling patterns. Mature seeds like this are most likely to germinate and thrive. Seeds that are a

kind of light green are mostly not

mature enough and have been removed

from the plant too early.

There's no harm in trying to make them

grow, but you may not have as much

success. When you've got a full-grown

crop, you could cultivate your own

cannabis seeds and you don't need to

deal with anybody in the future.

Chapter 3

Growing Cannabis

Obviously having seeds is just the first step in a long line to complete so that your cannabis plant can begin to grow. You need to know where the growing would actually take place before you start doing it. There are of course, two key options: indoors and outdoors.

Cultivating cannabis is not like buying up

bags of pumpkin seeds in the grocery store and simply tossing them on the field. Many marijuana growers need to take stock of the viability of growing marijuana in the region they have been granted. For example, do you have the room in your home to grow marijuana indoors? How many plants would you want to grow? Are you willing to be a grower with all the vagaries? If you cultivate weed outdoors, do you have a secure location? What's the weather like where you live? How's the soil going? These issues and much more will be discussed in the following portions of this book.

Section 2 Indoor growing

Chapter 4

Indoor Growing

Indoor weed production is the only

option for many citizens. Fortunately,

cannabis is a moderately polyvalent

plant which can produce several

varieties indoors and outdoors.

However, you can consult with the

breeder and see where they are

supposed to grow their plants.

Breeders often develop plants

specifically for outdoor use.

The last thing that you want to do is cultivate indoor marijuana plants that are primarily for the great outdoors. If you cultivate your marijuana plants in correct conditions, you will generate about a pound per square meter of marijuana. Temperature, air flow, humidity and plant treatment must be ideal, however when grown indoors it can be managed very well.

No extremes in weather or cat in your neighborhood that would threaten your cannabis.

Chapter 5

Lights

The life blood of plants developed indoors is always lights. Due to the scarce essence of any sunshine, artificial light is precious and essential. Photosynthesis, which is necessary for processing of sugar and tissues, requires light for plants. Many who grow for personal use have constructed their garden in a wardrobe. Some people will use a bedroom that is not obvious from the outside and that is never otherwise utilized. Any cultivator must, therefore, determine if there are significant numbers of lamps, both in terms of room and electrical power.

The majority of farmers prefer one of three light types: LED, Fluorescent, and HID (high intensity) lights. Light choice is a hot topic among growers, but I would suggest HID for the cheap entry point relative to a quality LED if you have enough space and cooling ability. These are marketed as HPS or Metal Halide lamps Although their upfront costs are greater than fluorescent or inflammatory lamps, their net worth is far larger on a long-term basis. Since they don't use too much electricity, they are brighter, and they last much longer. Though with a quality LED such as a Quantum dot board the lack of bulb replacements can save you money over time so be sure to factor in your specific situation.

So MH and HPS lights reflect a much

better value and a better overall

product. Plants would also require even

light distribution to ensure congruent

growth. A track device that enables the

light to be transferred can be hooked

up. This method is utilized by several

skilled cultivators.This way without

additional lighting here and there the

plants receive the maximum amount of

light. Frequently growers use

fluorescent lamps in germination while seedlings have an HPS light bulb. They don't create much heat and can be lowered to the top leaves around four inches away. Reflective material also leads to improving the light obtained by plants. It can be as quick as covering the walls with aluminum foil or just painting a bright white on the walls of the building.

Mirrors definitely do not show as much light as most materials and should not be used. Broad indoor gardens (and the light they need) put a certain amount of heavy burdens on the electrical power. Personal farmers would not have any issues, since they can only use few hundred volts every hour, contributing a cost of $10 to the electric bill. In the other side, extensive producers could be constrained by their circuit scale. For example, older homes can have just a

15-amp circuit that cannot keep all the

light needed by a wide garden.

Chapter 6

Germination

You should initiate the germination

phase as soon as the lights are up.

Germination basically means taking and

sprouting marijuana crop. The seed would stay just a seed for the near future if you do not offer it the required setting. Several approaches may be used to germinate the pot seeds and each grower suggests something else. Most of the solutions are restricted to the use of soil (or other rising media) or a wet towel. Looking only at these possibilities, soil tends to be the most natural way to germinate seed. Please position the seed in the soil approximately 3mm thick, then retain the soil humid for 7 days. This typically has a success rate of about 75% to 80% in terms of seed germination, which relies mostly on seed efficiency. The wet paper towel technique is reasonably straightforward and allows you to put the seed on a moist towel and fill it over the top. The success rate with this procedure is in principle, roughly 80 to 90 percent, but breaks during transplantation are more popular. The seedling obviously won't grow on a towel, and thus transplantation is a must which should be carried out with much caution.

Other possibilities for germination are "propagation kits" which is basically a fancy and more cost-effective way of saying "cropy media of seeds." This instrument can be found in several garden centers. But maybe the easiest

approach is to use just soil for any

novice. It won't be necessary to

transplant because it is the most natural

way for your seeds to germinate

properly. You run the risk of "shocking"

plants when transplanting the seedlings

at this early age.

It can either stun or ruin your seed, so

it's worth carrying on using soil until

you're comfy enough to use something else as a grower.

Chapter 7

Germination soil

This poses a simple question: "What soil can I use for germination?"In many garden centres, soils are particularly sold as "germinated soils." There is not really much

to differentiate them from more traditional soils except that they have certain nutrients and no manure. Pick the soil with a ratio of around 5:1:1 or 8:4 NPK (Nitrogen-Phosphorus-Potassium).

Currently, any soil consisting of a greater amount of nitrogen than the two other nutrients would be sufficient for sprouting weed seeds. Buckets that accommodate up to 2 to 5 gallons and typically used by farmers since the root structure of a marijuana plant can become very large.

For the germination and seedling cycle, smaller containers may function, but the plants will have to be transplanted later. It makes sense, then to cultivate the pot seeds and to hold them for the remainder of their lives in a single 2- to

5-gallon bucket. This helps the roots to expand and flourish in an ideal habitat for nutrients and a satisfactory water reservoir. Furthermore, it's easy to hold them in the buckets. The plants would require between 25 and 35 watts per square foot based on the strength of the lighting you have. The seeds do not need light to germinate instantly, but farmers typically start turning the lights after seeding the soil into a soil warm and germination-friendly climate. It is good to have the lights on and ready as the first sprouts start coming out of the soil. The pH equilibrium and real soil texture are just a couple other aspects that you can take into consideration. Throughout the entire life of the plant you are allowed to use the same soil if you guarantee that it drains correctly (texture) (between 6.0 and 8.0). The texture is especially critical as neither dry nor too wet soils should be. Moist, almost wet, soils decrease the quantity of oxygen that enters the root. The soil should be fine as long as the roots can "breathe" and hold ample water intake.

Chapter 8

Light Cycles and Distance from Plants

Probably the greatest part about

growing marijuana inside is that nearly

any element of the growth process is

regulated. While the seeds themselves

may not initially require light, as they

develop detectable sprouts they

definitely need light. Light functions in

this time as their sustenance which may

influence the plants later in life if they

are robbed of the precious light they

need. This clearly implies the adequacy

of soil, nutrients and irrigation systems.

The lights should be close to marijuana

plants at this delicate point. It is optimal

to carry fluorescent lights down to about

4 in away from the soil. At about 16 to

18 hours a day the light period should

also be reasonably rigid. This would be

the light period for much of the plant

life, but a stable timetable can be challenging to sustain. You should buy an automated timer that costs just about $8 and you can concentrate on other things. Some plants may use a more intense light regimen depending on the individual strain. Cannabis is simply willing to consume light, since it is a dominant herb. Some cannabis farmers have started providing their plants with 24 hours of light as opposed to 16 or 18. Most growers may not have to hit these extremes, but if you want to boost growth, you will need to raise the light period to over 18 hours often. The automated light timer will make things even simpler and certain lights can easily be mounted with a timer. The light can always stay as near as possible to the plants, as the cannabis plant ages and continues to grow, without risking harm to them. The light directions may tell you to hold them at a certain distance

from the plants, but a lot of light energy

is required to grow cannabis. In reality,

you can position the light around 2 to 4"

away from the tops of the leaves.

Chapter 9

Watering

All life on the earth needs some sort of water, but extra care should be practiced while dealing with cannabis.

Stop flooding the cannabis plant with moisture throughout the germination phase.

It is advised that the top layer of soil be wet, although even then only a few water sprays from a spray bottle are ideally used. The field around the stem should be kept dry until the plant actually germinates. This is because wet situations across the stalk will also contribute to redness. It's reasonably simple to overwater marijuana plants at this point (and at any level). The use of excess water can trigger significant soil problems and seed stress. The soil should not be too wet, as described above. In reality the roots can drown due to the lack of oxygen as you render thesoil soggy by overwatering it. This is especially valid when tiny seedlings in large pots are watered.

These plants should to be sprayed as many as larger plants so they don't have to take as much water. Sadly, if you overwater the plants will be impossible to determine because the signs of overwatering and underwatering are the same (i.e. the leaves will droop). (i.e. the leaves will droop). Of course, the soil moisture level is tested by one way. This can be achieved easily by treating the dirt. If the soil is moist, it's better to keep the plants on to irrigation.

Whether it is already certainly damp it would still have enough of water to pull from in the ground. When the soil is dusty, it is probably advisable to apply more water. As the plants expand, more and more water is required to quench their thirst. In general, it would not be ideal for plants to leave the soil unusually damp or exceedingly dry for some long period. Indeed, it must actually be damp and dry in order to allow better ventilation of the soil. Tap water is also used to plant marijuana, but many farmers complain about its viability. Any urban water supplies are utilizing a great deal of chlorine to destroy beneficial bacteria. The plant outside. Chlorine would usually not be a big concern and many plants will flourish and develop with chlorinated water.

Solutions for fish ponds are normally

used but may be used to create a

marijuana garden. Basically, the parties

involved apply sodium to the tap water

they intend to water. Sodium attaches

to sodium chloride with chlorine in

water (a.k.a. salt). It may not damage

the vine, but if used heavily, the water

source can become too salty, too and

some miners, recognized as hard water, will be poisoned.

During a lengthy period of time, while hard water will damage your plumbing, it will not have a detrimental impact on plants. The minerals in the water directly lead to development by providing additional nutrients. During the increasing season, it is desirable to remain away from artificial water suppressants since they appear to place excess sodium in water that renders the

soil and plant unhealthy. They also use

certain other artificial additives which

might not be useful for the plant

afterwards

Chapter 10

Indoor Vegetative Growth

As soon as the marijuana plant exits the

seedling point, it will become vegetative.

The growth rate will rise through springs

and limits, and with time more leaves

and branches will emerge. The plants

are like real marijuana plants. Hopefully,

they can start.

Chapter 11

Transplanting

Marijuana plants which have been germinated in tiny pots would have to be transplanted into larger ones until vegetative development begins. If the containers for plants are too little, they may be rootbound and lose vigor easily (or even die). Naturally, it is important to transplant before that arises. The transplanting phase should be handled with great concern, as a consequence of the regular transplant shock. If you handle the procedure with excessive attention, you may prevent transplant shock. Make sure that the soil is damp before you do it, because nothing is jarred. Place a spade in then In the soil

about 1" out from the stalk of the plant

(or a broad spoon). Make sure you don't

hurt the roots and take away a clump

big enough to complete the transplant.

A hole should be planned in the fresh

soil beforehand. Squeeze pot upside

down Beware of rootbound Nearly

Rootbound Put the plant in the pole and

cover it as well as you can with the fresh

dirt. You may take it off so that the seedling is at the same height.

The soil is moisturized to allow a nice melting phase for transplantation and the host soil.

You will not need to think about the plants withdrawing from any transplant shock as you do this properly and correctly and will begin to develop normally. When the first root tips emerge from the bottom of the

container, I transplant my plants.

Chapter 12

Vegetative Growth Techniques

The plants will spend their lives in the

vegetative stage of development from

now on.

At this point, it is crucial to ensure that

you build all the right atmosphere

conditions for development, higher

yields and higher potential. One of the

advantages of indoor weed is

Who without taking natural forces into

consideration, you will exploit the

circumstances precisely as you see fit.

Chapter 13

Water and Lighting

Essentially, we've already seen how plants should be handled and how much light they should get. During vegetative development, plants are likely to get "thirstier" and need more water as they become larger. The same principles also exist when it comes to watering: do not significantly overwater and do not be severely underwater. Many growers are creating patterns for watering their cannabis plants. For example, one day you might water, avoid watering for two days, and then water again It just just depends on the plants themselves. For a few days, you ought to pay careful attention to just how dusty the soil gets. If the soil is already damp, so you will be able to stay with the same pattern, but if it dries dramatically until the next scheduled irrigation, you can raise the rate at which you water the pot plants. As it comes to light, weed takes a lot of watering. In reality, it is possible to hold

the lights on 24 hours a day to reach the

optimum growth potential. Adjustable

light tracks are perfect if you have a

large growing space and no electricity to

switch the lights around to any area of

your yard. This way, every plant is

provided extreme quantities of high-

quality light. Try to keep a close eye on

the space between the lights and the

top of the canopy, 20 to 30 inches is

normally ideal. The rapid pace at which the plants appear to expand would allow them almost everyday inch closer to the lights.

So, make sure to position the lights near enough to have ample light energy, however far enough away that the tips of the leaves do not flame. If you choose to prevent this you can add an air-cooled or water-cooled device that will reduce the heat generated by the lamps.

Most of the aspects about electric light bulbs is that they generate both light and heat once they are switched on. Of course, if you let them go unburdened, they might generate extremely high temperatures.

But if you want to maximize use of all the light that they have to provide the cooling device would help the lights to get closer and perform easier in the long run. It can also be remembered that certain lights produce various color spectrums. If we speak of visible light, we're talking about all the shades we can see that are also described as ROYGBIV (red, orange, yellow, green, blue, indigo, and violet). Marijuana has a potential to flourish under illumination that is high in the red spectrum. This encourages photosynthesis, which is essential for the development of tissue during vegetative growth. High-pressure sodium (HPS) lamps emit the most light

in the red continuum (and the most light

in general) and are often the better

option in nearly any point of the rising

phase. Using something that is high in

the green continuum, wilted,

unproductive plants will usually be

grown. This is largely because the plants

completely embody green light, which is

why they are green in color themselves.

Making sure you check my website

every now and then to get the new

strategies for growing marijuana.

Chapter 14

Soil Control

When you have an indoor marijuana

garden, soil is often a relatively

significant factor to keep an eye on. It's

something you have more power over

too. As mentioned above, cannabis tends to thrive in a nutrient-rich soil with a neutral pH of about 7.0. However, often the pH in the soil will change very far away from the comfortable range of 6 and 8 on the scale.

Any extreme steps will need to be done to guarantee that the soil does not end the life of the plants. One approach to eliminate chemical pollution in the soil is by using a soil flush. In general, this is not a suggested move to take, but could

be appropriate in certain circumstances.

In fact, it can only be used as a last

resort when you attempt to keep your

marijuana plant alive. Essentially, it

means taking the whole plant with the

pot included and throwing it in the

drain. From there, turn on the faucet

and let the water flow through the soil

to remove all of the pollutants that may

have been harmful to the plant. The

danger of this approach is that you run

the same risk of destroying the plant by

oversaturating the soil with water as you

do by contaminating the soil with so

much nutrients. Although occasionally

this is the best way to make sure that

the additives don't destroy the pot

plants. There are also solutions for less

serious problems. If the soil pH

decreases below the recommended 6.0

and becomes too acidic, you should

easily apply some lime to the soil every time you water it. The pH should be restored to the appropriate range between 6 and 8. If the soil is above 8 and too alkaline, you may suggest adding a concoction of cotton seed meal, lemon peels and ground coffee. Some fertilizers are often made to be strongly acidic and will reduce the alkalinity if added to the soil. In any scenario, it's still a smart idea to keep testing the pH balance of your soil, else

you could be in for a surprising surprise.

Chapter 15

Nutrients and Feeding

Of note, the main cause of any

significant soil pH anomalies is the exact

nutrients that you add to the soil. Unlike

utilizing normal earth, the soil has to be

infused with nutrients. Often you can create a sufficient volume of nutrient only by having a special mix of fertilizers. But in certain situations, you'll need a solvent to "water in the nutrients. Of course, if you inadvertently add too many nutrients, you could end up rendering the soil poisonous (which would cause one of the soil control procedures laid out above). Skilled growers tend to feed their plants with about 6 pH of water. In any case, all plants require nutrients to survive, and supplying them with these nutrients will make sure that your work pays off in the end. "NPK" (Nitrogen, Phosphorous, Potassium) has already been listed as the three main nutrients that any grower requires to recognize. During vegetative development, the fertilizing solution should be one in which the concentration of N is greater than or equivalent to both P and K. Again, if you like, you can assist with a nutrient infusion by using a fertilizer. Fertilizers can to a large degree, be combined with soil prior to the start of the growing period. In general, though, you will find remedies that can be used to "feed" the vine. In certain instances, the plant would not need to be fed as much as possible. In reality, you just need to feed it once a week if all is going well.

However, you can never feed the plants with 100% of the nutrient content since the marijuana plants "burn" quickly. Instead, dilute the solvent to about 50 percent so that you don't have to use a soil flush. Certain essential chemicals include Calcium (Ca), Magnesium (Mg) and Sulfur (S). In general, it can be challenging for you to note any significant differences in the amount of nutrients that plants take or do not take. In reality, in most situations, the absorption of nutrients is the least of your concerns. As long as the soil is healthy and you choose to follow the same food for your nutrient solutions, you should be all right. Most farmers have a few diluted solutions on hand to make growing a little simpler. One solution can be an NPK solution where N has the maximum concentration. This is to be used for vegetative development.

Another solution should be NPK in which P has the largest concentration (used for flowering stage). You should still hold a few bottles of diluted micronutrient solution in case your plants really want to turn around. Nutrient shortages can kill your marijuana plants and significantly reduce production.

Chapter 16

Pruning

Pruning pot plants can be both logistical and helping to grow more buds when it comes to harvesting time. Many indoor growers would want to hold their plants in control if they start rising too high.

This is because there is just so much

vertical space in the growing room that plants can actually extend their wings. Indoor plants, for the most part, do not grow as big as outdoor plants, so they would need to be kept at bay once they start developing very well. Snipping off the top stem would also cause the plant to produce further branches and to expand wider. So, although you might be dropping vertical height, you're not going to sacrifice much in terms of girth.

If your aim is to ensure uniform growth, then cutting shoots and leaves will not really damage the plant if achieved in moderation. You don't want to get too carried away by this when you're cutting too many Shoots and leaves will make it hard for the plant to develop. You've had to allow it some time to regenerate before chopping off a significant number of leaves or shoots. For many farmers, this can sound like a waste of perfectly acceptable leaves and shoots, but during vegetative development, shoots are the most potent component of the plant. They will generate a high-quality smoke that will at least make you a little buzzy. The leaves may also be used for cooking preparations with great results. The pot plants on the photo on the right are produced using a process named ScrOG. It's an advanced growth strategy, but it will double the yield! Although it can sound obsessive, the vegetative growth period involves intricate attention to detail on any aspect of plant production. Neglecting any one factor could end up with negative consequences on your plant's capacity to survive and grow an outstanding bud.

Chapter 17

Air

As with most living things, fresh air is incredibly beneficial. Opening a window or adding a fan device in the room will help to give your plants some much-needed fresh air. Of course, if it's especially cold outside it's definitely not a smart idea to leave the window open for too long, even if it's the only way to recycle the air. The cold outside can

stunt the development of the plant and

make it impossible for you to help them

recover.

Chapter 18

Temperature

The temperature of the growing room and the plants is also something that needs to be controlled and managed. The average temperature for the rising room should be about 75*F. Yet weed is surprisingly adaptive and can grow buds of lower or higher temperatures. If the temperature declines to severe lows or increases to extreme peaks, you might be shocked when it comes tothe condition of your plants. While cannabis will thrive at temperatures about 50 to

55*F, it will not

yield the finest, most potent weed when

it comes to flowering and harvesting. In

general, maintaining the room at around

75*F is your best option. In fact, plants

can develop somewhat faster at slightly

higher temperatures, but it can be

challenging to sustain these higher

temperatures. You will still need to

mitigate the excess heat by watering the

plants further to cool down the roots.

Often when it comes to temperature

maintenance, lights create a challenge.

Lights that generate a lot of heat will

make the room feel swollen and cause

the plants to dry up or burn. If this is an

issue, you might want to add an air-or

water-cooled device to reduce the heat

generated from the lamps. If you need,

you can also add an air conditioner if it's

cost-effective for your rising space. Most

homes can maintain average temperatures about the optimum, so it is vital for you to track the temperature on a regular basis to ensure that your plants are properly maintained.

Chapter 19

Humidity

You might think about humidity as something that happens in the Deep South or in other tropical environments. But humidity can be found almost anywhere, including your rising space. In general, about 40 to 80 percent of the relative humidity (rH) is optimal.

Humidity is simply a calculation of the water in the climate. This can to a large degree, be accomplished by utilizing fresh air as mentioned above. Some growers also have a RH meter at their disposal to ensure that the perfect percentage of humidity is properly tested. There are also costly machines called dehumidifiers that regulate the humidity levels in a room. Still, unless you're planning a very substantial operation, you may only be able to get away with a little fresh air once in a while.

Chapter 20

Carbon Dioxide (CO2)

Another essential ingredient that plants need to thrive is CO2. For humans, CO2 is not that nice, but plants like cannabis

use CO2 as their air. It's literally the sort

of thing that makes them breathe. Yet

CO2 is also essential to promote and

sustain photosynthesis. If your rising

room needs adequate CO2 supply, it is

likely to become evident. There are a

number of methods to increase CO2 in a

space, but the best way to do it is with a

CO2 generator. These generators will

maintain a constant supply of CO2

flowing into the room, and the plants will be able to take it right away. There's really no way to inundate pot plants with CO2 unless you somehow get overboard somehow. For example, if your rising space is dangerous for you to breathe, you may need to tone it down a little. Otherwise the volume of carbon dioxide in the room is directly proportional to how high the plant (and later the buds) can expand.

Chapter 21

Flowering

Because you plant indoors the period
the plants begin to flower is almost
exclusively based on whether you
choose the plants to flower. Of course, if
the buds are the most potent, you want
to start flowering. It is necessary to hold

a marijuana plant in a vegetative

condition for up to

10 years, although these plants would

definitely not be potent at the end of

their lifetime.

Until you cause flowering, you'll

definitely want to know which plants are

male and which plants are female.

Chapter 22

Determining the sex

In general, the plants can appear to "pre-flower" before you can even manipulate them to flower.

During this time, they will begin to display subtle indicators of their sex. Male plants typically begin to pre-flower sooner than female plants (around two weeks). This will show itself in male plants becoming taller than female plants. They could even grow bags that look like buds, but they're not buds. The explanation why male plants grow quicker and taller than female plants is because they can pollinate them. The pollen in the sacs (or fake buds) will drop to the females to begin the pollination process. By comparison, the female plant will reach pre-flowering by developing white, hairy growths at the nodes and at the top of the cola (the head). They're called pistils, and they're what draws the male pollen to the female plant. There's still no sure-fire way to ascertain sex before they start displaying these telltale signs. You may however, take a cut from one of the plants and then grow it in a region different from your yard. The cutting is actually a clone of its "mother" plant which shares the very same genetic structure. You will then compel the clone to bloom, and it would certainly

begin to display signs of its specific sex.

Then you can go back to your garden

and mark any plant you're doing this for.

Many growers choose to decide sex as

soon as possible, since the female plants

would naturally yield a much better

height. It's not to suggest that the males

are worthless, but you just want to draw

a difference

between the male and the female at an early point, so that you can go on with information. This is particularly true of growers who want "sinsemilla" buds.

Sinsemilla simply means "withoutseed," in Spanish, because if the males are not permitted to pollinate the females, they may not generate any seeds. These seedless female plants are significantly more potent than their peers because they rely more on the development of

THC and bud growth than on the production of seeds. In reality, you can virtually see the THC resin slipping off the buds. Of course, this involves the early removal of male plants. If you're depending on your own garden to send you seeds for next year's crop, this actually wouldn't be a smart idea. As described earlier, purchasing seeds from a dealer or even a seed bank is always a random pick-up bag. You don't know what the seeds would be and receiving a complete batch of males is not outside the scope of possibilities. Allowing the male plants to pollinate the female plants will give you lots of seeds and you won't have to pay for them. It is also likely to wind up with hermaphroditic plants, which are actually only plants with both sets of reproductive organs. Thus, early indicators in both male and female plants can be seen. Most farmers often exclude these plants from their crop, even though they wish to pollinate the females. Although self-pollinating, they can only ever grow hermaphroditic plants, and might also pollinate certain non-hermaphroditic plants. It may sound like the best of all worlds, but understand that the effectiveness is often reduced when it comes to these plants. It can also be remembered that male plants are not worthless when it comes to smoking either. They can also yield a little bit high and can even be used in culinary preparations. It's really necessary to exclude male marijuana plants if you choose to cultivate Sinsemilla. One male marijuana plant can pollinate hundreds of females.

Chapter 23

How to Force Flowering

Now that you know how to look for the signals of male and female plants, the next move is to get them to flower properly. Only note that if you start to blossom, it might be hard to interrupt the flowering. The males can pollinate the females if you haven't removed them. Even if you divide the plants by sex, the air could still bring some of the pollen to the female pistils. It's just a tossup on whether you want hyper-potent buds for this year alone or whether you want to keep developing your favorite strain without having to pay for fresh plants.

(Most personal growers would prefer to adhere to the above choice because paying for their own seeds every year may be costly).

In any case, if you want to compel flowering, all you have to do is place the plants on a 12-12 light regimen. That simply means you're going to have to keep the lights on for around 12 hours a day and switch them off for the other 12 hours. Although the space can be kept as quiet as practicable throughout the 12-hour cycle of darkness. Switch off the lights won't often do the trick, particularly if there are other light sources nearby. In reality, even though a spotlight shines on the plants for a few minutes at a time during the dark season, it will hold them in vegetative growth. If you have windows in the rising space, do your best to block them out, particularly if the sun rises before the 12-hour cycle is over. If your lights come with a timer, so it's a smart idea to configure it so you don't have to think about changing the lights on and off every 12 hours. You will find that the female plants will continue to grow larger as the flowering cycle starts to expand. They will grow more leaves, buds, and bulbs, and the plant will start growing more THC overall. It will begin to take on a kind of cone form that resembles a Christmas tree, and you might also begin to detect a distinct fruity or smoky smell. Their pistils can shift from a white color to a darker hue (usually brown, red, or orange) and at that stage, they should be ripe for harvesting. Even if you want to pollinate the female plants, you might think about

eliminating the male plants from post-

pollination so that the female plants

have more space to survive. The plants

tend to bloom when the light and dark

cycles are identical at 12 o'clock since

they are genetically conditioned to do

so. If you plant outside (more on that

later), you can find that the plants tend

to bloom naturally as the daylight begins

to dwindle in the fall. (Note: There

would be a segment on the harvesting

and healing of the plants below since it

is the same method for both indoor and

outdoor growing).

Chapter 24

Indoor Hazards and Pests

In certain situations, indoor growers

would not have to think about any

pathogens or pests plaguing their plants.

But it doesn't imply it's unlikely. In

general, microbial diseases are limited

since microbes that impact plants

typically do not occur in Europe or North

America (where it is possible that many

of you will grow). Nutrient disorders

exist, but they are only times where

plants obtain too much or too little

nutrients. This can be remedied in a

variety of forms illustrated in the

"Indoor Vegetative Growth" segment above.Pests are mostly what you need to work on avoiding or removing once they find their way into your home. This is because in nature, these bugs can be mitigated by their natural predators, but in the sealed system within your home, they will have none but you to deter them. Of note, avoidance is still the safest choice when it comes to these species. Yet some of the more insidious plant bugs, such as mites and whiteflies, are very difficult to spot. You should place them in your hands or clothing, or they could fall through cracks in the windows. It's quite likely that the mites might have been in your house to begin with. Most houseplants are immune to certain forms of pests, but that doesn't guarantee that the pests remain away from the houseplants. Indeed, if you have a houseplant that is immune to mites and other rodents, it could already be infested with many of these animals. You will try this by bringing a weed seedling in a jar with the other houseplant. If the seedling begins to display symptoms of drooping or enervation, or if the leaves tend to turn white, then you possibly have mites already in your house. Be sure you never use the same equipment for your houseplants and your marijuana garden.

If you have windows in your rising space, add a nylon mesh or wire barrier to deter pests from accessing it. Often make sure that the soil you use is pasteurized and thoroughly sterilized such that it does not contain any larval eggs. Pests can be devastating to the pot plants. If you believe any intruders in your rising room will act instantly. There is a segment of my website about pest management with pictures of all potential pests.

Chapter 25

Eliminating Pests

If you ever incur an infestation of mites or white flies (or some other pests), there are a few measures you can do to

get rid of them. Of course, insecticides

are going to work, so many people don't

want to damage their plants with all the

chemicals involved.

If the plants are otherwise safe, but you

can see any significant decay in the

leaves, you might want to force

flowering right away. If only a few plants

or a few leaves become affected by the

pests, then attempt to eliminate the

infected parts. Plants that are already in the flowering period are likely to hold up to any pests adroitly. If the situation continues, you may want to ask about the usage of an insecticide. Sprays that contain products like pyrethrum, rotenone, and malathion

are usually deemed healthy for plants when correctly used. Of course, you don't have to spray a whole insecticide canister on your plants to get the job done. The greatest aspect of these insecticides is that they dissolve to chemical substances such as CO_2 and water when they quit functioning. There are natural remedies that you can produce, but they're not as good as insecticides. However it is necessary to eliminate any infected leaves before spraying, and also not to use any insecticide during flowering.

Chapter 26

A Few Indoor Security Notices

While most people grow indoors to prevent security concerns, there are still some problems that may happen if you're not cautious. In certain states, cultivating pot is also undoubtedly illegal, and if an unfriendly snitch feels there's a cause to believe that you're growing up, you might end up behind bars (or at least paying a hefty fine). The first law regarding growing marijuana is not to worry about growing marijuana.

And if you feel like you're friendly with your neighbor or bank teller or acquaintance, they may not be friendly with the activity of growing pot. While it's normal for any gardener to want to warn everybody about their exploits, it's risky when their gardening plant happens to be unlawful. The first law regarding growing marijuana is not to

worry about growing marijuana. And if

you feel like you're friendly with your

neighbor or bank teller or acquaintance,

they may not be friendly with the

activity of growing pot. While it's normal

for any gardener to want to warn

everybody about their exploits, it's risky

when their gardening plant happens to

be unlawful. If you have a window in

your growing space, it won't be that

easy to cover pot plants unless your window isn't open to your neighbors or someone else from outside. Often if you left the growing lights on at night, anyone may be prompted to suspect that something suspicious is going on. To stop this you should purchase a blackout curtain that can be drawn back much of the time you spend cultivating weed. A blackout curtain can also also making the cultivation process smoother, since it means that no

outside light is leaking. Often the pot

plants send off the characteristic scent

that you associate with cannabis. It may

be a reasonably powerful wave out of

some open window. The fragrance can

render your neighbors suspicious,

particularly if they are not proponents of

cannabis cultivation. In this situation,

you may need to hold your window

securely closed and add fans in the rising space to circulate the breeze.

Section 3 Outdoor growing

Chapter 27

Outdoor growing

Many farmers choose to sow their weed seeds outdoors because they're meant to have a healthier smoke and there's definitely nothing more natural than cultivating the plants outdoors. Any of the environmental considerations outlined above would be given to the plant by natural resources that you would not have to supply yourself with.

Although indoor growing offers you a lot of flexibility, outdoor growing encourages plants to thrive to their maximum potential. The only drawback with outdoor growing, though is that

plants are noticeable to anybody who

happens to have prying eyes. If you live

in a suburban area, you may be able to

get away with growing your plants in

your backyard, but you're likely to need

to be very paranoid about holding the

operation under wraps. And though, you

may already be captured, and the fines

are theoretically very severe unless legal

in your jurisdiction. If you live in a

secluded or wooded area and own a lot of ground, it may be a little simpler to cultivate your own smoke on your own farm. For example, if you live on ranchland (or have connections to a friend's ranchland), you may be able to grow successfully outdoors with limited interruptions.

This is the perfect way to do it so you can check plants anytime you want without risk of getting detected. You should still escape the difficulties of

coping with criminals trying to score

your homegrown bud. Unfortunately,

many citizens may not live in legal states

or have proximity to secluded private

property that does not give rise to

scrutiny from law enforcement or other

individuals. A system known as

"Guerrilla Farming." This ensures that

you're going to have to travel to public

lands that are kind of off the beaten

track to expand your garden to the best

of your abilities. There are apparent

risks of doing this, that someone might

happen in your garden and warn the

appropriate authorities. It is also not

rare for law enforcement to survey

certain public lands using helicopters or

slow-flying aircraft. The police are fitted

with infrared sensors to track any

vegetation anomalies. If the location you

planted in your garden is accessible, the

plants are likely to be easily noticeable to everyone flying in. But if you plant underneath some thick vegetation, it might just blend in with the rest of the trees and shrubs in the field.

Chapter 28

Soil

No matter where you grow outside, healthy soil is a must. But not all kind of soil is going to be perfect for cultivating the marijuana. It's a smart idea to evaluate the soil on which you want to

develop before you really need it. This is

to guarantee that it would not be either

alkaline or acidic as the plants continue

to stretch their roots any deeper to the

earth. If the pH test moves very much in

any direction, you may want to try a

different spot, or infuse the soil with

some nutrients and fertilizers. Many

farmers might want to use compost as a

natural fertilizer. Anything that used to

be organic should be used as manure.

This ensures that you can harvest leaves, banana peels, and even dog drops, and in a couple of months, you'll have a good, nutrient-rich fertilizer. You can't, of course, only take the leaves or shrubs or banana peels and use them as fertilizer if they haven't decayed. But nearly every decayed organic material renders a cheap fertilizer. You will purchase other fertilizers from the supermarket as well. Fertilizer with an

NPK ratio of around 5:1:1 (just as

before) would be the best alternative.

Any fertilizer that contains more

nitrogen than the other two nutrients

would be suitable for much of the

plant's existence before it blossoms

when more phosphorus is ideal. Of

instance, if guerrilla farming is your

favorite form of agriculture, then you're

not even going to have these choices at

your disposal. In reality, once you have a definite position selected months ahead of time, you just won't have the luxury of making a more workable soil. You're just going to have to go with what you can find, because walking in your own fertilizer could make it all the more obvious that you're growing something out there. Sowing SeedsMany growers like starting out their seeds with rows that are fashioned into the soil. You don't even need to bury the seeds that

are deep in the dirt. In reality, some

farmers have been reported to only

disperse their seeds to the top of the soil

to get them to germinate. This random

seeding is called broadcast seeding.

Maybe a more efficient method to have

the plants sown is by the use of hills or

mounds. Essentially, you sow the seeds

on the tops of the small mounds in the

soil. It definitely allows you the freedom

to plant outside and though the soil is a little muddy. This is because, of course, the water is going to drain off the moundSo that the seed (and, later, the plant) would not be inundated. In either a hill or a row, strive to ensure that the seeds have some sufficient soil coverage so that they can remain damp. Most guerrilla farmers use broadcast seeds to limit any suspicion and make things a lot simpler. If you spend hours constructing rows or mounds, there's a high chance that anyone could happen to you. It is also unusual to have some sort of uniformity in nature. If the plants are ordered in perfect rows, or they're all sitting on a tiny mound of some sort, so any passersby (whether on the field or in the air) would certainly note the phenomenon. Scattering the seeds around certainly gives the field a look of utter arbitrariness as nature may have expected. The plants will mix in with all the other scattered trees and/or shrubs and will not be readily seen by someone else. Unfortunately, broadcast seeding is not the only way to guarantee that the plants germinate. If you put a coat of soil over your seeds and softly push it down to the soil with your foot, there is a greater possibility that the seeds can germinate. Many seeds, however, will never germinate or actually die after being seedlings if you attempt to

develop in this manner. That's why it's

important to use a significant volume of

seed for broadcast seed so that you are

ensured some development by the time

they start to germinate.

Chapter 29

Germination

As with indoor germination, outdoor seeds need moisture to germinate properly. Using too much water may be dangerous, but as long as the seeds are reasonably loosely moisturized, they can start to germinate. Of course, this is better if you create mounds or rows to hold the seeds very damp. Often outdoor conditions are not conducive to germination or the subsequent seedling level. If you live in an environment where temperatures stay very low in the spring, you will need to germinate the seeds indoors. To do this, only obey the guidelines set out above in the indoor growing segment on germination. You will then implant the seedlings as the weather begins to change. Again, transplanting to a secluded position on public property is at best, futile and at worst, risky. There is a high possibility that the plants will not withstand the transplant because of all the tension they're facing. There is still a high possibility that you will be captured, so it will actually take more than one trip to place all the plants in the right location.

The entire germination phase is difficult for guerrilla farmers, particularly if there is no reliable source of water nearby. Hiking in your own water could be difficult, but the soil would also need to be moist for the seeds to germinate. If you're curious, learn all about weed guerrilla cultivation.

Chapter 30

Weeding:

As your plants begin to germinate, it's essential to keep the area free from weeds. Stop utilizing some weed killers including Round-Up that could harm the pot plants as well. It should be remembered that weeds can end up taking a lot of water and fertilizer for your plants if you don't stomp them out quickly. Although the fastest way to get rid of weeds is literally by pulling it by hand. Trying to destroy them with some chemicals is only going to be bad for the plants you want to develop to be healthy and powerful. Obviously, before planting in a field, you can eradicate any weeds that happen to be there The advantage of being outside is that you don't actually need to think too much about light. The sun is going to supply all the light a plant might like, plus even more. There's no way to reproduce the power of the sun, because it's such a greater light source than something you might artificially make. If you transplant your plants from indoor artificial light to outdoor sunshine, they might be surprised by the intensity. This would definitely not be the best way to start your outdoor growing experience, since you could see the plants losing their vigor and inevitably die. If you sow the seeds outside in the direct sunshine, the plants will be acclimated to the heat for the remainder of their lives. And then when transplanting from indoor to outdoor, put the plants in a place that is shaded for part of the day to continue by ensuring that the sun's rays reach them specifically but for a shorter period of time. This is assuming that you leave them in portable containers rather than planting them directly in the field. When they continue to get accustomed to the sun's rays, they eventually shift further towards strong sunshine until they obtain light every day. This method does not take longer than 7 to 10 days to get the plants acclimated to sunlight. Light may even be a concern if there's anything that stops you from getting to your plants. For example, if you reside in a gloomy place,the plants can not obtain enough sunshine. You will need to carry the plants inside at night and place them under some lights so that they get a complete complement of light during the day. If you are a guerrilla farmer in a forested environment, then the plants may be in danger of getting obscured by higher trees in the area. While trees offer protection and shelter for future spectators, they can also restrict the amount of light your plants get. It's going to be hard to transplant them once they're in the field because you might just have to live with the small amount of light. If planting on the hillside, make sure you're planting on the south side of the mountain (if you're in the northern hemisphere). This is how the sun is moving from east to west, so it's going to be in the southern half of the atmosphere. If the plants are on the southern slope of the ridge, they can get as much sunshine as possible during the day.

Chapter 31

Watering

your outdoor plants can be tricky, particularly if they are situated in a very dry and arid area. If your plants aren't close to a hose, so you're going to have to formulate a scheme to extract as much water as possible from your plants. Obviously, early on the plants may not require anything in the way of H_2O, however once they undergo vegetative development and continue to develop much bigger, they will need more water. Large adult plants will drink up to a gallon of water a day. This doesn't mean you're going to have to spray the plants with a gallon of water a day, so the soil can hold some of the water from the prior watering's (or even rains). If your plants are on private property that you have access to, there is no lack of special methods that you may use to bring water to your plants.

For eg, you can fill buckets with water and move them to the rising site with a truck. Try to prevent wasting and overflowing the water in a single plant.

Some farmers have set up a watering drip system that works more like a bottle of squeeze that has a permanent drip. This approach helps farmers to stop needing to water the plants every day while maintaining the soil moist on a continuous basis. Since by default it is incremental, the drip system holds the plants reasonably safe and does not overwhelm them with water. Of course, you might be living in an environment where cannabis will flourish naturally without the need of any additional water at your end. This is perfect for rebel farmers who are unlikely to be willing to inspect their plants on a regular basis. If you are a guerrilla farmer and you live in an environment where the weather is always hot and dry, you might need to hold a firm eye on the plants. Hiking in your own water is going to be challenging on a variety of occasions, and it's easier if you can locate a local lake or stream that can automatically supply you with water. If your plants are underwatered, they are likely to start wilting. Just be mindful that the plants would spontaneously tend to wilt in the summer as a reaction to the sun's heat. The easiest way to verify whether your plants have enough water is to dig about 6 inches into the dirt, make sure you don't cut any big roots down the path. If the soil is always cold and damp, the plants should be perfect. Many soils are adept at retaining water for a long period of time, such that there is effectively a pool of water built up there. If at all necessary, you would want to water your plants with a nutrient solution only once every few weeks. As long as the nutrient solution has a higher concentration of nitrogen than phosphorus and potassium, it will be fine for vegetative development. Using a solution that is richer in phosphorus than one of the other two nutrients for flowering. This is expected to be achieved at the time you water the plants.

Chapter 32

Temperature, Air

Obviously, temperature is one of the most critical concerns when planting outdoors. There's not anything you can do to keep the plants warm enough or cold enough to meet their needs if there's an issue with the temperature. If you have your plants or are already in containers, you should shift them inside to prevent extreme cold at night. When the weather is especially high outside the roots may start to "boil" in the soil. Holding them cool with extra water can help to guarantee that the plants do not begin to lose their vigor. Of necessity, being outside leaves the plants open for a huge range of other weather issues. Wind, rain and snow (depending on where you live and where you plant) will all be issues that damage your plants. In certain instances, strong winds would have no impact on stable hemp plants. They usually grow solid stalks that don't require any outside help to keep upright. Indeed most high winds may create any miniature fractures in plant stalks, however if they are stable, they can repair themselves very quickly.

But if plants suffer from nutritional

shortages, they can have a rough time

healing. This is also valid if the upper

portion is bulky and prone to more

angled twists of the stalk. In this

scenario, you may be worried of stowing

the plants so that they don't suffer any

irreparable harm. Whether you are

Knowing that the hurricane is imminent,

it's better to locate the weakest plants

to make sure they have some outside protection to minimize the harm that the storm might do. To do this, simply position the stake about six inches from the base of the plant, and then bind the plant and the stake together with the wire or string. It's a smart thing for rebel farmers not to place the seed on a slope known to suffer mud slides. Although not every slope is going to be a direct mudslide. A clear sign that the environment is not going to be adequate

for your plants is if there are no other

small plants developing in the area. If all

you see is solid trees or shrubs, the

slope is not likely to accommodate a

minimal vegetation. This might wash out

the whole crop during a freak summer

storm. There's nothing safer than the

great outdoors in terms of the air quality

that your plants can encounter. Your

plants will receive all the fresh air they

need and a lot of CO2 to remain safe.

Chapter 33

Outdoor Flowering

In most instances, flowering outdoors would need little feedback from the grower. Most plants begin to adapt to changes in the daylight hours and start the flowering phase. The days would naturally begin to get shorter, which will cause the flowering of the plants or for certain farmers, this will not be the perfect situation. Sometimes you don't expect the plants to bloom, and sometimes you want them to flower earlier. For example, if the weather is still good and you want to eke out all the vegetative growth you can with your plants, then you'll want to postpone flowering as long as you can. By the same way, if you realize that the temperature will quickly get extremely

cold or at least too cold for the plants to

thrive, then strive to make sure they

start to blossom earlier than they might

naturally have. Both of these choices are

feasible for farmers who have

connections to their seeds. If you want

to postpone the flowering phase,

it just needs a little light in the night.

You can do this with a high-powered

spotlight shone on the plants every few

hours or so for around 10 minutes in the night. This will sufficiently mess with the natural instinct of the plants to start flowering, and for the time being they will remain in vegetative development.

Chapter 34

Marijuana Flowers Outdoor

Obviously, if the weather begins to get cold early where you live, strive to make sure your plants start to bloom as soon as possible. But outdoor plants have several obstacles to this aim. If the time of light to night is not even 12 hours to 12 hours, so you will have to make that work on your own. Using a polyethylene board, it helps to block every sunrise or sunset light so that you can get the necessary 12 hours of darkness. For eg, if you realize that your field can obtain

precisely 13 hours of sunshine during

the day and that sunset is at 7 p.m., then

put the sheet over the plants at 6 p.m.

and remove it at 6 a.m. as the sun rises.

After around 1 to 2 weeks, the plants

should start to bloom and you can start

harvesting.

Guerrilla farmers are kind of out of luck

when it comes to exploiting the

flowering season. They're going to be at

the whim of the local weather in the city, and they're not going to have a choice in the matter. Only believe that nature is going to work its magic and find a way to give you some excellent smoke.

Chapter 35

Diseases, Predators, and Other Threats

You would expect plants grown

outdoors to do even

worse than plants grown indoors when

it comes to pests.

That's real, but since the environment is

mostly self-regulating, there are a

number of tricks to get rid of unwanted

tourists. For example, that though a few

bugs try to chew on the leaves of your

cannabis plants, it is possible that they

will be kept in control by all of their natural predators. Spider mites, aphids, white flies, and mealy bugs are all popular pests that many farmers have to contend with both within and outside. Plants are at highest risk when young and not well-developed.

A single meal for a community of mites, while the plant is a seedling, could do any irreparable harm to the plant. But when the plant grows, it may continue to become less vulnerable to enervation by the bites of a small insect. This is mainly because these larvae can be taken care of by natural predators before any harm is done to the plant. If pests are a concern, there are a few ways that you may use to keep away from your strategy.

Chapter 36

Companion planting

Although the THC created by marijuana

is intended to serve as a natural

repellent, sometimes it is not very

effective to get rid of those insects.

Many outdoor growers have taken it

upon themselves to plant companion

plants that function to eliminate any

pests.

In general, you have to cultivate

companion plants near the real weed

plants. The most powerful repellent

plants are those with heavy scents such

as cloves, herbs and mints. Garlic cloves

are definitely the strongest repellents

since they mean that a large variety of

pests remain away from your yard.

Aphids, spider mites, potato bugs,

several varieties of beetles, and a

broad variety of other rodents can be repulsed by garlic cloves. And rabbits and certain deer are going to be scared off by the presence of garlic cloves.

Mints are especially useful at containing flea beetles if you have a particularly big infestation. They even repelle a large array of other insects and also rodents.

Geraniums and marigolds may even be interspersed between the garden to offer an even broader spectrum of defense. Geraniums may also be placed outdoors in containers so that you don't have to go through the trouble of really growing them in the dirt. Marigolds are some of the quickest growing flowers and can develop a good fragrance in a matter of days.

Chapter 37

Natural Predators

You may even purchase the natural

predators of

these pests and put them in your

backyard. Some insects like ladybugs

have little pleasure in consuming a

marijuana plant, but they do have a lot

of appetite for aphids and insect eggs.

Praying mantises and lacewings often

offer you a natural way to rid yourself of

any unwelcome pests. They're mostly

distributed commercially. Several

animals, including blue jays, robins,

martins, chickens and others are adept

hunters when it comes to fighting off

pot bugs. Some farmers have built

birdhouses, feeders, and water pools to

draw these species. Nor is it a terrible

thing to allow a few chickens, ducks, or

geese run around the garden every once

and a while as the plants get larger.

These birds can remove a lot of rodents

along with a variety of various weeds,

and you won't have to do much job in

that regard. Some bug pests include

frogs, toads, spiders, turtles and lizards,

both of which should be allowed to live

in your backyard.

Chapter 38

Certain Repulsive Techniques

Many gardeners use some clever

homemade sprays

or other solutions that are surprisingly

efficient.

It is necessary to use a concoction made

of a liquid garlic extract and a normal

mixture. You should also incorporate

cayenne peppers, tomatoes, or nearly

everything else is healthy for the

marijuana plant and pungent enough to

repel several different kinds of pests.

If you just want a cheap workaround,

you can actually

either stumble on the glitches or

squeeze them to death.

It's better to do this early in the

morning, as the bugs usually travel much

slower. If anything it offers you anything

to do in the morning before you go to

work or do whatever you have to do for the day. A lot of growers want to put walls around their garden. This is especially successful for guerrilla farmers because it's hard to notice and it doesn't take a lot of time to plan. What you need to do is build a barrier about 6 feet away from the plant using powdered potash (wood ash). You should also spray some of the wood ash on the leaves to avoid the bugs flying in the harbor. Homemade spray

Greenhouse holds away a lot of pests.

Yet insects are not the only pests that

can create problems. This is especially

true if you reside in an environment

with a significant number of omnivorous

or herbivorous mammals or birds. Deer,

mice, rodents, pigs, and other animals

are vulnerable to seeking ways to get to

their pot plants. When the plants are

young, it is normal for the deer to come

and basically decimate the field. When plants mature, though, animals are not that drawn to it for large animals, the only repellent is

a similarly large barrier, however many farmers may not have the privilege of being able to construct a fence.

There is also a need for other strategies to drive these mammals away. Many farmers have been buying urine from such predators. For eg, whether there is a community of deer Is always playing around with your yard, so you might think of

buying some bear urine and putting a ring of stuff around the plants. When the deer catch the scent, they would naturally try to avoid the place from here on out because they know the smell as predatory. This may also function with smaller mammals. As long as you buy the urine from one of the major predators of the mammal, they'll

keep away. The rabbit may be repulsed

by the smell of fox or wolf urine. You will

buy these repellents in many outdoor

markets In general, birds are not a

significant danger to the garden of

marijuana. However, after you've only

planted the crops, crows, sparrows, and

starlings may

be potentially detrimental to your crop

because they like to pilfer the seeds.

They will be a concern in this respect

before the plant germinates and

becomes a seedling.

To keep some of your seeds from being

taken early, you might use plastic nets

or even a scarecrow to get the birds out

of your back. Since the seeds have

germinated, you're not going to have

any issues with birds.

They just don't like the flavor of a leafy

pot product.

As described above, birds should be

allowed to nest in

your garden since they are natural

predators of other insect pests.

Chapter 39

Any notes on outdoor defense

Obviously, the distinction between cultivating outside and indoors is that your plants are practically wide open to any spectator who happens to be walking by.

Whether you're on public property (or even private land), there's still a risk that the plants will be discovered either by law enforcement or by criminals. The only way to actually keep yourself from getting caught is to cover your tracks meticulously. If you're rising on public property, make sure to choose a spot that would be difficult to explore by land or air. Try to locate an area where you realize there are unusual or non-existent fly-bys. Also don't cultivate your garden in a place accessible from any paths or walkways. Even a random resident might report your crop to the authorities, and even if you don't capture it you're probably going to ruin your garden. It's definitely a smart idea to remain as clandestine as possible and to keep out of reach of any audience (for say, a park ranger) when you go to the greenhouse. If you can locate a spot that is secluded but not impossible to access, so you'll be much better off as you take care of your plants and eventually harvest.

If you have to go on a reasonably long walk to a location like a clearing in the trees, then it's important to take 3 or 4 separate routes to the place. Even an inexperienced tracker can begin to note the direction you take

as you walk to your garden if you only have one entry point. This route would be clear to any criminals

or anyone who know what they're searching for.

You're still going to want to quit your garden in a better direction than you come in. For example, if you're planting in a park with a variety of different paths, it may be wise to reach the park on one path, quit that trail to tend to your garden, and then leave the garden to get on another trail. Always have a chart of the land handy in case you get lost. Where necessary, consider accessing public property through unremarkable locations (for example, places that don't have trails). While developing

on private land, make sure you do all in your power to prevent the plants from being noticed. This involves pruning and trimming them so that they do not give rise to any distrust on the part of passersby or neighbors. Plants grown outdoors will also achieve enormous heights that render them reasonably noticeable to those searching for themselves.

For example, if you grow up in your backyard, a six-foot mutant plant would attract the attention of any neighbors relatively easily. Holding the plant pruned may restrict its size which detectability, and can also result in better yields in the end. Some farmers have proposed cultivating their crop on land next to their own, which is held by someone else.   For eg, if you're living next to a cornfield, you may think it would be beneficial to develop out there. Unfortunately, it's impossible to guess how

many homeowners check their property or land.

Whether there are any flybys in the region. If you get captured, plan to be slapped with more than one trespassing penalty. It can also be repeated that you should never speak to someone about cultivating weed.

And if your plants are highly isolated and almost difficult to locate, don't warn anybody.

Chapter 40

Harvest

Indoor and outdoor harvesting are practically the same thing, except that in the case of outdoor farmers, you have to

put the harvest indoors. If the plants are

on private property so you can only take

the plants out of

the field and move them to your home,

so you're not going to have any

problems. Guerrilla growers though are

likely to have to step in to retrieve their

plants and then walk out unseen. Of

course, this is usually not that simple to

achieve and can need the support of

a buddy depending on the nature of the plant and the total size of the crop. If at all practicable, aim to do something in the night or in the early morning to keep anyone from noticing you. And if you cover the plants in your pockets, every spectator can come to some clear conclusions. In any case, taking a few leaves and shoots until the real harvest season is one of the most sensible options you might make. This basically means that you'll at least receive

anything with all your work in the event

that your plants get ripped off or seen

by law enforcement. It's always ideal for

indoor growers

to taste a little smoke beforehand. In

reality, the leaves and shoots during

vegetative growth can be very powerful

and can give you some pleasant smoke

in general. The best moment to pick the

plants would not always be clear. You

don't want to harvest too early,

and you don't want to harvest too late.

On this scenario, the THC and other

cannabinoids on the

plant would not be as abundant as you

would like.

Obviously, if you want sinsemilla buds,

the male plants must be picked early

enough that they do not pollinate the

female flowers. If you pull the male

flowers early, you're not going to risk

too much in terms of potency or yield.

For the most part, male plants also

do not yield the best quality smoke.

Even, if you want to stop pollination,

you can have them out as soon as you

have sex. If you want to pollinate your

female plants, you can only leave the

males in the soil so that they can bloom

and generate pollen. This will prevent

you from trying to pick up the males

early, and it will also guarantee that you have seeds for next year's harvest.

When it comes to pollinated female plants, you're not going to want to take them out until the seeds have had enough chance to develop. Many growers are beginning to see the telling signs of strong THC output and increased flower and bud growth, and they may think it's a smart idea to take out their female plants. Although if you take the plants out too early, the seeds

will be inert and may not germinate until

the next season. You should look at the

seeds by opening up their sheaths or

bracts to see whether they have reached

a marbling brown color synonymous

with maturity. Of course, sinsemilla

plants do not have to rely on seed

maturation to render them viable for

harvesting. Although, typically speaking,

these plants have a longer flowering duration.

In reality, they may bloom for 4 to 5 weeks, with new growth occurring almost instantaneously. The new growth would be a kind of bonus to your total yield,

but you can wait before there is a significant decrease in flower quality.

This would usually happen in the fourth or fifth week of flowering. Don't start harvesting automatically when you encounter the downturn. Wait about a week after the fall begins to finally start harvesting your sinsemilla seeds. This is when the THC is at its peak, and the smoke is the most potent. If you leave the plants in to develop further, they will

slowly develop a little larger and generate a few extra buds. But the THC isn't going to be as strong because it's actually beginning to degrade. In order

to finally pick the seeds, what you have

to do is softly dig them out of the dirt.

You would want to damp the soil

beforehand to encourage this process.

Stop bending or cracking the plants

when you lift them up to render them

difficult to work with. If your plants are

in containers, you can easily take them

out or even drain the container and all

the dirt out. There are several various

methods for extracting and shipping weed.

Chapter 41

Activities post-harvest

When you actually harvest the seeds, the first thing you

can do is cut the fan leaves from the

vine. This is because they are less

potent than the colas, and they

therefore do not heal as quickly as the

other sections of the herb. However it

doesn't imply

they can't be included. In reality, the fan

leaves are known to have a very high

concentration of THC, particularly after

they have just been pulled.

You should start grading and manicuring the plants after you've achieved that. Grading essentially means distinguishing plants by their individual sex, strain, and anatomical portion of the plant. For example, you might position all sativa-dominant, female top colas in the same region. Many growers prefer to hang their plants upside down from a wire, if only because it's much simpler than doing something else. Manicuring means removing the extra leaves from across the colas so that the plants can dry very quickly. Once all the plants are neatly graded and manicured, you will start curing them if you wish to. Curing is a method that is intended to pull out the best tastes and tones in the grass, but often it will also minimize the amount of THC significantly if you're incorrect. Sinsemilla buds also do not need to be healed since they are as potent as they are. The most popular method to treat a plant is by curing the air.

It includes hanging the plant upside down in an unventilated space. You want the temperatures to be reasonably hot, because if you can put the plants in the light, the healing phase can go ahead without a hitch.

The plants tend to lose color and appear pale at which stage the ventilator or window can be opened to slow down

the curing phase. It will take you about

six weeks

to complete the full span of the remedy.

If you're experiencing relatively overcast

or rainy days, or if the room doesn't get

up close to 90*F, you may be at risk of

getting mold on your plants. This is

something that you desperately don't

want to happen, and you may want to

introduce a radiator of any sort to bring

the temperature up as far as it can go.

Flue curing accelerates the mechanism

of curing by introducing an additional

force that helps to heat the plants

quicker.

You should put the plants in a water-

tight box

that is then positioned in a tank of water

(generally, a fish tank). Then heat the

pool with water to around 90*F

consistently. When the plants begin to

lose their

green color, switch the heat to around

100*F.

When all the green is eliminated from

the plants, crank the heat up to 115*F

again. This method may often dry the

plants, however, make sure to switch

the heat down when they continue to

dry, or they will end up becoming brittle.

This procedure usually requires about

about a week to complete. Sweat curing

is a procedure used mainly in Colombia

to cure plants within around 5 days.

In general, stacked branches and colas

are around 1.5 feet wide and 2 square

feet minimum. The microbial activity

acts like a fermentation mechanism in

the same manner that the manure

continues to heat up. Plants are

beginning to lose color bit by little. You

should pick out the plants that have lost

the most color every day. To prevent

mold or decay, put paper towels, cotton

sheets or rags between the plants. The

rags can trap some extra

moisture to allow the curing process

smoother.

Chapter 42

Drying up

You should start drying your plants at

this stage.

Drying is a required operation,

particularly if you

want to store your bud for later usage.

It reduces the possibility of incurring mold and

therefore, means that the grass lasts a long time.

Many farmers use a slow drying process that essentially includes hanging them upside down and enabling the air to dry out naturally. This normally takes about two weeks to finish. Of course, they may often continue to cure a little during this phase, which may somewhat reduce the potency. Quick drying methods require the use of the refrigerator, the use of the microwave and also the use of the skillet. Most people may want to evaluate their weed reasonably quickly, and while these approaches can yield a harder overall flavor, they will also give you the chance to smoke some weed shortly after harvesting. It should be remembered that you do not want to dry the whole harvest using either of these fast-drying processes. In reality, it could be more advisable to dry plants using a heater to promote the normal slow drying method. In any case it is necessary not to leave the grass in the oven or skillet for too long. Hold it in the oven for around 10 minutes at a temperature of between 150 and 200*F. Don't be reckless as you might end up charring your bud.

Chapter 43

Housing of commodities

Storing the bud is the safest way to

guarantee that it survives until at least

the next harvest. Many growers simply

position their dried bud in a dark

(usually

glass) jar and then placed it in the refrigerator or freezer.

Light and heat are two of the most critical factors that can degrade THC, but if you leave the storage area dark and cool, you will always be able to enjoy the cigarette in the future. It can also be remembered that storing the whole crop together is a catastrophe formula.

While it may be more practical to do so, you

also run the risk of incurring mold on the

plants.

If any one part of one plant remained

wet, you might end up ruining the whole

mold harvest. That's why it's necessary

to hold your crop separate such that you

don't end up in a tragedy like that After

that you can still plan for next year's

crop by tilling any soil or testing your

seeds. Of course, you should only kick back, rest and appreciate the fruits of your labor for a bit. Luckily, this Grow Bible has guided you through the beginning of increasing your pot flower, and it will continue to support you when you keep developing for years to come.